P9-DVJ-149

Georgia
on my mind

FALCON™

Copyright © 1990 by Falcon® Publishing, Inc.
Helena, Montana

All rights reserved, including the right to reproduce any
part of this book in any form, except brief quotations for
reviews, without the written permission of the publisher.

Design, typesetting, and other prepress work
by Falcon®, Helena, Montana.
Printed in Korea.

Library of Congress Number: 90-55232

ISBN 1-56044-027-9

For extra copies of this book
Please check with your local bookstore, or write to
Falcon, P.O. Box 1718, Helena, MT 59624.
You also may call toll-free 1-800-582-2665.
Visit our web site at www.falcon.com

FALCON®

Dogwood trees shading the tumbling cascades of Upper Dukes Creek in Chattahoochee National Forest near Helen   DAVID MUENCH

introduction

For as long as I can remember, I've always felt the spirit of a place. A profoundly romantic notion, of course, but I'm not ashamed of it. I picked up the notion during my college days at Mercer University when I first read the nature poems of William Wordsworth and Samuel Taylor Coleridge. But who hasn't had the same experience? You go for a walk in the woods, and suddenly the landscape becomes startling—leaves rustle their small tongues, the river whispers over rocks, the foliage breathes out a particular fragrance. Soon the place comes to possess its own personality, its own spirit. Making such connections with places can move us in powerful ways, and in Georgia the various geographic regions—the salt marshes of the coast, the pine and red clay of the mid-region, the green mountains of the north—are all ripe with possibility.

I was born and raised in Cherokee County, about forty-five miles north of Atlanta in a region where the foothills first start to climb into the Appalachian Mountains. What I remember best about the town of Canton in the 1950s is the simplicity and innocence of the place. It was the archetypal American small town. I lived with my folks by the side of Georgia 5, the highway to Atlanta, and my mother's parents lived in a converted garage apartment behind us. My father's parents lived across the highway, two hundred yards to the north. They ran a small grocery and dry goods store, and their fifty or so acres comprised the primary geography of my childhood—a baseball field my father built, a horse barn and

Brown thrasher, Georgia's state bird   JAMES H. ROBINSON

pasture, two chicken houses, and several lots full of hunting dogs.

My first experience with the spirit of a place was in the woods above those dog lots. Whenever I needed mystery and adventure, I hiked up a long hill to an old, bent oak. It was one of the largest trees in those woods, and the middle of its trunk had grown into a strange and tilted Z—bent by the Indians, the story went, to mark the way to a place I could only imagine. Maybe that was just a tale; I had no way of knowing. But it didn't matter. The truth I knew was the feel of the place, the spirit of it manifested in the mystery.

Sometimes, too, this spirit showed another side of itself. I remember being up there one afternoon in late summer when a storm churned up over the ridge. The woods darkened, and thunder broke so hard the ground shook. I didn't even think about shelter. I just stood there in the rain, listening to the thunder and watching the limbs of the oak sway. The place had taken on a different feel—almost as though the spirit I had grown to know had suddenly fallen into a deeper, more somber mood. I don't know if this was the first time I became aware of the way weather colors our sense of place, but I haven't forgotten the experience, and I haven't ceased to watch for those changes now. The seasons and the different shades of character they bring to a place always fascinate me—the sun and thunderstorms of spring and summer, the cool rain of fall, the cold sleet and occasional snow of deep winter.

Part of the mystery and presence of those woods also had to do with the birds and animals I encountered on my walks—a squirrel circling a pine trunk to hide from me, a rabbit in the field beyond my grandfather's dog lots, a mockingbird lost somewhere in the trees, a vulture sweeping the edge of a clearing. A few places I knew as a child even seemed to possess a spirit dominated by a certain animal. The pond below our house seethed in an atmosphere that seemed to ooze up from the earth—the ominous spirit of the copperheads that lived by the hundreds on its bank. But there too I found the spirit of the fish—the bass feeding in the shallows, the catfish wallowing in the depths, the crappie, the sunfish, the bream, all the various fish that embody the mystery we constantly need to dredge up out of the depths.

Other people feel this in other places, I know, and there are states in this country that have larger areas of wilderness. But these are not comparisons I make when I'm in the woods or on the water. I watch for whatever

Jefferson Davis, Robert E. Lee, and Stonewall Jackson riding forever across Stone Mountain, east of Atlanta
CRAFTON MARSHALL SMITH / THE IMAGE BANK

the place will offer me—swamp or marsh, river, lake, pine woods—the creatures are there, always wholly sufficient and various. In fact, Georgia has as varied a wildlife as I have seen anywhere—from wood stork to alligator, mourning dove to mule deer, a wealth of spirits impossible to catalog.

When I was in college, several landscapes in Macon also held spirits for me. One was a place I knew simply as "The Grotto," a beautiful ravine of dogwoods and wildflowers rumored to have once been the site of a monastery. Because it meant trespassing, I only visited this spot a few times, but I hold a vivid picture of its colors—purples, yellows, deep reds, a scattering of dogwood pink—abstract and shifting in the wind. Something about the way the light sifted through the needles and leaves, the smell of the honeysuckle, the deep silence of the gorge, made everyone I took there feel a special presence. Sometimes it was so eerie and overpowering we had to leave. Other times it was deeply peaceful, comforting. But many places in Georgia have a similar effect on people. I think it has to do with the tremendous variety and abundance of wildflowers and flowering trees, which make many spots in Georgia seem like great wild gardens.

My wife, a native of the Northwest, felt this shortly after she moved here and discovered magnolias and dogwoods in bloom. She spent whole days walking around our neighborhood investigating the flowers. This isn't a strange reaction for a first-time visitor. Indeed, the spirits of many places here express themselves with a startling vocabulary of color and fragrance.

A place in Macon I visited more frequently was Rose Hill Cemetery. I remember it especially at night—dark, rolling hills sloping toward the Ocmulgee River, marble tablets and crosses, angels with broad and sometimes broken wings, brick-walled terraces of grave slabs, and mausoleums all gray in the moonlight. I remember also the clusters of hardwoods scattered over the hills and the shadows they cast on bright nights, and I remember one brick wall that overlooked the railroad tracks and the river. In the late sixties, this is where I went to commune with the mysteries of the cosmos.

To some people, thinking of a cemetery as a beautiful place may seem slightly strange, but Rose Hill in Macon, Oakland in Atlanta, and many other cemeteries throughout Georgia *are* beautiful. There is no other word to describe them. They combine sculpture, architecture, and history, all in one landscape, and in doing so they make a profound statement about the way we seek to order our lives and culture.

History, of course, brings a unique and defining spirit to any place, and one of the things I've always loved about Georgia is that constant and pervading sense of the past—I almost want to say the immediacy of the past. By this kind of spirit I mean the atmosphere sensed when the characteristics of a landscape are overlayed with its history—the knowledge that James Oglethorpe traded mules with Tomo-Chi-Chi in that very bend of the Savannah River, or that on a single afternoon in 1864, ten thousand men met agonizing deaths charging that particular face of Kennesaw Mountain.

Being a native Southerner, I was made painfully aware of history from an early age. But the feeling for this kind of spirit inhabiting a place—this notion that the past fuses somehow with a landscape to be felt with it in a single sensation—didn't become a conscious preoccupation of mine until I was in my late twenties. Like most Southerners of my generation, I've always been fascinated with the War Between the States (as my grandmother insisted on calling it), and whenever I had the chance I liked to explore the local battlegrounds. My favorite was Kennesaw Mountain, where a greatly outnumbered Confederate army tried desperately to block the Union advance into Atlanta. One night on the mountain I almost got lost in a dense fog. I remember an odd feeling as I watched the white clouds sifting through the trees and brush, and suddenly I felt as though the spirit of the place was showing itself to me—cool and vaporous, seeping up through the leaf-cover, manuevering across the mountain.

Of course, this idea is entirely romantic and relies on the sensibility of the observer. But what aspect of the world doesn't? The fact of the matter is that history maneuvers all over Georgia. The first European settlers here were Spanish soldiers who hit the coast around 1566. They had come north from St. Augustine to set up a post on St. Catherines Island. The English made their claim in the 1730s, when James Oglethorpe shipped over boatloads of colonists to settle on the Savannah River and founded the city of Savannah. But over the next forty or so years, Georgians, like other colonists, began to think of themselves as Americans, and the spirit of that revolution still can be strongly felt in Savannah, Augusta, and other coastal towns.

Several years ago I visited a beautiful home in Savannah. It was one of those old row houses that dated from colonial times and was listed on the National Register of Historic Places. I remember the atmosphere in the house as we had a wonderful southern dinner of baked ham and fried chicken in the elegant dining room. Except for the electric chandelier and the air conditioning, it might have been colonial Georgia. The spirit of the times pervaded the place. Later on that evening I was told that the house was one of several in the area with a "documented ghost" from the Revolutionary War. I don't remember anything of him, or perhaps her, but I do know I sensed something of a presence that can be felt in many Georgian cities, a history that seems to seep not only out of the monuments in the parks, but out of the streets, the trees, the very bricks and boards in the old houses.

Savannah, a city of parks and flowers, is as beautiful physically and as fascinating historically as any city in the South. But Augusta and Macon deserve equal acknowledgement in those respects. And Macon, in fact, may have a greater wealth of ante-bellum homes than any other city I can think of—on his march to the sea, Sherman stopped at the Ocmulgee, lobbed one cannonball into Macon, and turned east toward Savannah.

Of course, when the first Europeans settled here, Georgia was already inhabited by numerous tribes of Native Americans, some living in highly civilized societies. Perhaps the most advanced culture belonged to the Cherokee, who by the late 1820s had established a written language, were printing a newspaper, and were translating and printing books. Their history with the state of Georgia is a sad one and ended, for the most part, in 1838 when what was left of the Cherokee nation was herded west to the Indian territories along the infamous "Trail of Tears." These were the people my ancestor John Benjamin Bottoms lived and farmed among in the early 1830s, and they were the people who occupied my imagination whenever I visited that twisted oak in my grandfather's woods. But there were many other Native American cultures whose loss was just as tragic, and several beautiful places in the state still bear witness to their creativity and spirituality—Rock Eagle near Eatonton, the Etowah Indian mounds near Rome, the Ocmulgee mounds in Macon, to name only a few.

Unfortunately, there are other terrible sins in our history—the worst being slavery. But they have left spirits that teach and heal us. Who can go unmoved after visiting the Martin Luther King Memorial? Most Georgians have developed an interesting and healthy attitude about history, based in no small part on the Old and New Testaments. Like Southerners as a whole, they seem to understand that humanity itself is marred with imperfection; we make mistakes, but if we're wise we learn to profit from them. And we are, for the most part, wise in this respect and have shown ourselves time and again to be visionary and progressive.

The city of Atlanta is a perfect example. Burned entirely to the ground by William Tecumseh Sherman, it has grown to be the unchallenged capital of the Southeast—the unparalleled leader in business, education, and the arts—home of Coca-Cola and Delta Airlines, of Emory University, Georgia State University, Georgia Tech, Atlanta University, Oglethorpe, Agnes Scott, home of the Atlanta

Watching the Georgia Day Parade in Savannah   STEVE BISSON

Symphony and the High Museum. On top of this, Atlanta is truly a beautiful city, blessed with an almost infinite variety of good spirits. Of all the cities I've visited, I can say honestly that this is my first choice as a place to live. I love the architecture, the music, the galleries, the museums, the theaters, and all the other cultural wealth, but I also love the abundance of wooded areas, a resource not usually found to such a degree in large cities. In fact, the U.S. Forest Service recently reported that Atlanta is the most heavily wooded urban area in the country. This isn't hard to believe. My first piece of advice to any visitor is always to take a drive through a few of the neighborhoods—say Mid-town, or Virginia Highlands, or Emory. Then find a spot that looks inviting, park the car, and hit the sidewalk. In some neighborhoods there's just so much green, you can hardly see the houses. It's almost like walking in the country.

This is a distinction we're proud of, and it isn't something that many of us take for granted. I heard on a local television news program that woodlands in Atlanta are being cleared on the average of fifty acres a day. The story centered around a two-hundred-year-old red oak that stood in the path of a new MARTA rail line. The program included pictures of school children marching around the huge trunk of the tree, protesting and waving signs, trying to save it from the bulldozers of a construction crew. The issue was complex, and the people I talked with had differing opinions about what might happen. At question, though, was money, a lot of money, and so the oak came down. This is the dilemma of progress as we have defined it for too many years. But because of the good work of the Georgia Nature Conservancy and other environmental groups, Georgians are coming to understand the need to stop thinking of progress only in terms of development.

Appreciation, conservation, the willingness to change for the good of the place—these are the things we learn from the places that touch us. If we love the natural beauty of our state, we don't take that beauty for granted. If we respect our past, we don't overlook its blemishes, and we look forward with hope and anticipation to an even better future.

Of course, the spirits I feel here, the connections I make, are entirely my own. But everyone who experiences Georgia will find his or her own places—on the unspoiled beach of Cumberland Island, in the deep gorge of Tallulah Falls, at Stone Mountain, the King Memorial, Franklin D. Roosevelt's Little White House in Warm Springs—and each place will hold more than enough power for every visitor to make a connection. Landscape and history, the spirits are here in great abundance, manuevering constantly, ready for whomever will discover and take delight in them.

David Bottoms
Atlanta

Azaleas in full bloom ANNIE GRIFFITHS BELT

* *Georgia is beautiful. High on the crests of the Great Smoky Mountains some Almighty hand shook out this wide and silken shawl—shook it and swung it 200 glistening miles from the Savannah to the Chattahoochee, 400 miles from the Appalachians to the southern sea. Red, white, and black is the soil and it rolls by six great rivers and ten wide cities and a thousand towns....* *

W. E. B. DuBois,
These United States

Cloudland Canyon State Park, 2,000 acres of canyons, woods and waterfalls near Trenton   LARRY ULRICH

Bald cypress lining the banks of the Suwannee River near Okefenokee Swamp DAVID MUENCH

View from the top of Amicalola Falls, a 729-foot cascade—Georgia's highest—near Dawsonville   DAVID MUENCH

Aptly named leaves and berries of an umbrella plant   JOHN M. HALL

Fire pink, also known as catchfly for its ability to trap insects   JOHN M. HALL

13

Horsechestnuts dominating a dense forest in the Blue Ridge Mountains, northeast Georgia   JOHN M. HALL

> **"** *The sun was now below the horizon and the red glow at the rim of the world faded into pink. The sky above turned slowly from azure to the delicate blue-green of a robin's egg, and the unearthly stillness of rural twilight came stealthily down about her. Shadowy dimness crept over the countryside.* **"**

Margaret Mitchell,
Gone With the Wind

Sunset from Tesnatee Gap in the Blue Ridge Mountains, along the southern end of the Appalachian Trail, Chattahoochee National Forest   DAVID MUENCH

Immature red-shouldered hawk surveying its Georgia woodland WILLIAM S. WEEMS

❝ *Many people have concluded that Appalachia has something [simplicity] the rest of the country needs.* **❞**

Jim Wayne Miller,
A Mirror for Appalachia

Brilliant fall colors in the Appalachian Mountains DAVID PERDEW / STOCK SOUTH

The skyline of Atlanta from Bedford Pine Park   ANDRE JENNY / STOCK SOUTH

" The South is the future. It's the future right now. "

James Dickey

Staircase to the sky, the Georgia-Pacific Building in downtown Atlanta   MICHAEL W. THOMAS / STOCK SOUTH

The atrium at the 15-story Omni Hotel, Atlanta   JOHN ELK III

Past and present in Atlanta   ALAN D. BRIERE

" *In the South, the present seldom breaks clear of the past.* "

John J. Putman,
A Good Life in the Low Country

Southern belles on parade, Fourth of July, Atlanta   WILLIAM SCHEMMEL / STOCK SOUTH

Rhett and Scarlett look-alikes   DAVID MURRAY JR. / STOCK SOUTH

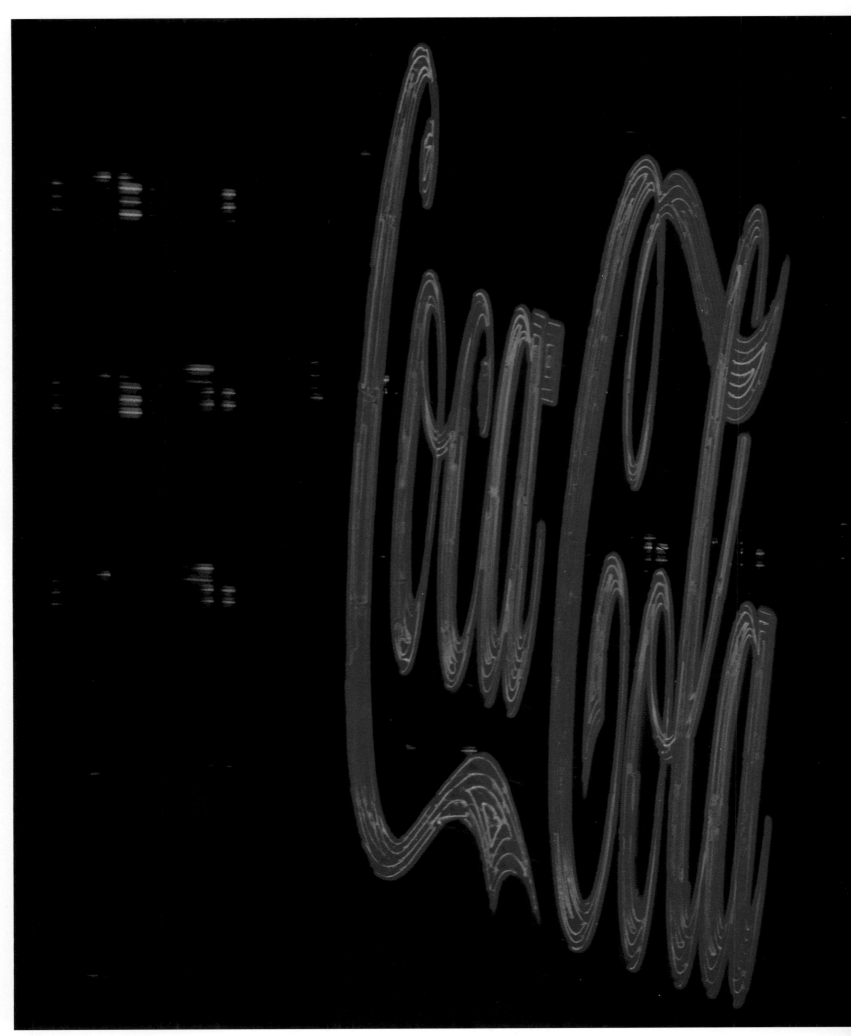

Signs of Atlanta—the dome of the state capitol, built in 1889, and Coca-Cola, invented in 1886   FLIP CHALFANT / THE IMAGE BANK

Happy to sell Coca-Cola CATHERINE KARNOW

Atlanta skyline   DON SPARKS / THE IMAGE BANK

" Atlanta is an upstart. A lusty country lass has come late to town, with lace on her parasol and red clay on her petticoats. Wise, now, in the ways of the world; a rich girl, a sophisticated lady wheeling and dealing and playing with the world's great and near great, who come courting in endless streams. "

Anne Rivers Siddons,
Go Straight on Peachtree

'57 Thunderbird cruising past the Buckhead Diner, Atlanta   MICHAEL W. THOMAS / STOCK SOUTH

Red taillights of a departing MARTA rapid train stretched cut by slow-speed exposure   ANDRE JENNY / STOCK SOUTH

Braves outfielder Oddibe McDowell sliding back to first DAVID PERDEW / STOCK SOUTH

Ted Turner at an Atlanta Hawks game DAVID PERDEW / STOCK SOUTH

Hawks' Kevin Willis blocking Boston's Larry Bird   DAVID PERDEW / STOCK SOUTH

"The region, topographically, was like a palm leaf, the Savannah was the stem, large at the bottom and gradually spreading out into veins at the top. On the side of the valley the creeks ran down like the depressions in the palm leaf, while between them lay the ridges of sand hills, like seams, and on the crests of the ridges were the tobacco roads."

Erskine Caldwell,
Tobacco Road

Sunrise over the Savannah River inlet,
Fort Pulaski National Monument   DAVID MUENCH

The historic Savannah Cotton Exchange, built in 1887 ED COOPER

Part of Savannah's historic landmark district, largest historic district in the United States   DAVID MUENCH

Pitching to a new generation, Whitfield Square, Savannah   KEN HAWKINS / STOCK SOUTH

Day's end along River Street, Savannah   JOEY IVANSCO / STOCK SOUTH

" *Savannah: The name begins with a whisper and ends with a sigh, inciting dreams of a never-never South, of belles and balls, soft accents and gentle courtesy, magnolias and Spanish moss, and all the rest.* "

Anthony Wolff,
American Heritage

Peach blossom CUB KAHN

Ballet in Savannah RALPH DANIEL

City Hall in Athens, the "Classic City"   ANDRE JENNY / STOCK SOUTH

❝ *God has not put any limit on what we can do in Georgia.* **❞**

Jimmy Carter

Jimmy Carter, former U.S. president and permanent resident of Plains, with Ethiopian peace team leader, Dr. Ashegre Yigletu   DAVID MURRAY JR. / STOCK SOUTH

Dancers at Macon's Cherry Blossom Festival, held annually in March   WILLIAM BERRY / STOCK SOUTH

Enjoying the sight and scent of some of Macon's 100,000 cherry trees   JAMES H. ROBINSON

Cotton boll ready to be picked FRANK OBERLE / PHOTOGRAPHIC RESOURCES

*"   . . . the magnificent quiet of a summer day when the heat is
intense and one is so very thirsty, as one moves across the dusty
cotton fields, that one learns forever that water is the essence of all
life. In the cities it cannot be so clear to one that he is a creature of
the earth, feeling the soil between the toes, smelling the dust thrown
up by the rain, loving the earth so much that one longs to taste it
and sometimes does. "*

Alice Walker,
In Search of Our Mothers' Gardens

Judging some of Georgia's finest at Cordele, "watermelon capital of the world" WILLIAM S. WEEMS

Flavorful handful at Ray Farms near Glennville MICHAEL A. SCHWARZ / STOCK SOUTH

King family portrait with Martin Luther King, Jr., as a boy (right) MICHAEL W. THOMAS / STOCK SOUTH

He gave us back our heritage. He gave us back our homeland; the bones and dust of our ancestors, who may now sleep within our caring and our hearing. He gave us the blueness of the Georgia sky in autumn as in summer; the colors of the Southern winter as well as glimpses of the green of vacation-time spring.

Alice Walker,
Writing about Martin Luther King, Jr., in
In Search of our Mothers' Gardens

Martin Luther King, Jr., Center for Non-Violent Social Change, Atlanta   MICHAEL W. THOMAS / STOCK SOUTH

King family home, birthplace of Martin Luther King, Jr., on Auburn Avenue in
Atlanta   MICHAEL W. THOMAS / STOCK SOUTH

Ebenezer Baptist Church, where Martin Luther King, Jr.,
was pastor   LAURA SIKES / STOCK SOUTH

Sand dollar on Sea Camp Beach, Cumberland Island National Seashore PAT TOOPS

" *...the wild horses prancing through sea oats on the majestic dunes...dazzling flocks of gulls soaring with sea liberty...the virgin beaches and the surf, thundering with the rhythm of eternity....These, the special properties of the sea islands, were a closely guarded secret of the spirit...* "

Betsy Fancher,
The Lost Legacy of Georgia's Golden Isles

Sea oats cresting a dune, Cumberland Island National Seashore   DAVID MUENCH

Palmetto frond ANDRE JENNY / STOCK SOUTH

Hikers on Cumberland Island National Seashore, where no cars are permitted
MATT BRADLEY

Live oaks draped in Spanish moss along the Georgia coast   DAVID MUENCH

" *. . . live oaks. They are the most magnificent planted trees I have ever seen. . . . The main branches reach out horizontally until they come together over the driveway, embowering it throughout its entire length, while each branch is adorned like a garden with ferns, flowers, grasses, and dwarf palmettos.* **"**

John Muir,
A Thousand-mile Walk to the Gulf

Laughing gulls soaring effortlessly along the coast of Blackbeard Island   ALAN D. BRIERE

Local transportation on St. Simons Island   DAVID PERDEW / STOCK SOUTH

Beach walking, St. Simons Island   WILLIAM SCHEMMEL / STOCK SOUTH

> *I don't know of any place where human beings coexist so happily with God's creatures.*

Charles Kuralt,
Dateline America

Blooming wisteria beckons beyond a boardwalk in Okefenokee Swamp Park   GENE AHRENS

Portrait of a bullfrog   ALAN D. BRIERE

Fragrant water lilies in 396,000-acre Okefenokee National Wildlife Refuge   DAVID MUENCH

One of Okefenokee's 15,000 alligators ANNE HEIMANN

Wood duck   JOHN HENDRICKSON

Suwannee cooter basking in the sun, Okefenokee National
Wildlife Refuge   JOHN HENDRICKSON

    Nowhere in the swamp, it seemed, was there a bird that simply went chirp; they grunted and gurgled, croaked and groaned; they rattled and made barnyard noises—oinks and moos. They managed to sound like rusty hinges and creaky screen doors.

William Least Heat Moon,
Blue Highways

Pelicans off the Georgia coast   WILLIAM S. WEEMS

Eastern newt, voracious predator of worms and insects   JOHN M. HALL

Hooded pitcher plants, insect-eating residents of Georgia's low pinelands, marshes, and bogs   JEFF LEPORE

Palm leaves along Georgia's southern coast KEN HAWKINS / STOCK SOUTH

Whitetail fawn   LYNDA RICHARDSON

66 *The colors of spring are cool colors—a million different shades of green, the golden-greens and gray-greens and silvery green of the young hardwood trees and the deep almost-black green of the pines.*

And under this overlay of many-shaded green lies the white of the dogwood, scattered on the steep mountain slopes like old snow.

When the sun shines and the wind blows, the whole surface of the mountain shimmers with many colors, like an opal in firelight, and sometimes the great bulk of the hills looks like the surface of a sunlit sea. 99

Harold H. Martin,
A Place in the Mountains

The second waterfall on Daniel Creek, Cloudland Canyon State Park   LARRY ULRICH

Toccoa Falls plunging 186 feet on Toccoa Falls College campus   TOM TILL

Pickerelweed blooming in the shallow water of Okefenokee Swamp   DAVID MUENCH

Damselfly   JOHN M. HAL_

" It is good to realize that, if love and peace can prevail on earth, and if we can teach our children to honor nature's gifts, the joys and beauties of the outdoors will be here forever. "

Jimmy Carter,
An Outdoor Journal

Dwarf iris, fragrant flower of Georgia's wooded hillsides and ravines   WILLARD CLAY

Princess tree, Blue Ridge Mountains   WILLARD CLAY

❝ He was singing a hillbilly song that sounded half like a love song and half like a hymn. . . . The sun was going down and the sky was turning a bruised violet color that seemed to be connected with the sweet mournful sound of the music. ❞

Flannery O'Conner,
A Good Man is Hard to Find and Other Stories

Plying the quiet waters of the Chattahoochee River in Atlanta, the "Big A"   RALPH DANIEL

Clematis   STEVEN Q. CROY

Magnolia blossom   KAREN LAWRENCE / STOCK SOUTH

Columbine   JOHN M. HALL

       Already summer was in the air, the first hint of Georgia summer when the high tide of spring gives way reluctantly before a fiercer heat. A balmy, soft warmth poured into the room, heavy with velvety smells, redolent of many blossoms, of newly fledged trees and of the moist, freshly turned red earth.

Margaret Mitchell,
Gone With the Wind

Tupelo and cypress along Cedar Creek, Okefenokee Swamp   DAVID MUENCH

Bobcat resting easy at Oatland Island Education Center, Savannah   KEITH LONGIOTTI

Providence Canyon State Park, Georgia's "Little Grand Canyon," near Alpharetta   GENE AHRENS

Landing Georgia's state fish, a largemouth bass   ERWIN & PEGGY BAUER

Competing at Callaway Gardens Resort near Hamilton   DAVID PERDEW / STOCK SOUTH

Sailing off St. Simons Island, one of Georgia's "Golden Isles"   DAVID PERDEW / STOCK SOUTH

Georgia rivalry, the University of Georgia versus Georgia Tech   SCOTT CUNNINGHAM

Some of the 25,000 runners in Altanta's annual Peachtree Road Race
cooling off under a rainbow   WILLIAM SCHEMMEL / STOCK SOUTH

The 15th hole during the Masters Golf Tournament at Augusta National Golf Course   STOCK SOUTH

Peachtree Golf Course, U.S. site for the Walker Cup
Amateur Tournament   STOCK SOUTH

Face-to-face with a spicebush swallowtail caterpillar, showing the large, eye-like markings that discourage predators   JOHN M. COFFMAN

" ...Autumn in Appalachia—a land of trees—is a must season for the visitor. We live in poetry all around us. "

Jesse Stuart,
Holiday

Maple leaves brighten a run in the Appalachian Mountains WILLIAM S. WEEMS

" *No matter what part of this forest you explore, there is something special about walking into these backwoods. It is possible to feel that you are the first person that has ever been here, especially on an autumn day when the wind blows through dead leaves and cascading water rushes over the stones.* *"*

Kenny Rogers,
Kenny Rogers' America

Autumn splendor in the Chattahoochee National Forest
near Blue Ridge   DAVID MUENCH

Maple leaves blazing with fall color, Cohutta Mountains in northern Georgia KAREN LAWRENCE / STOCK SOUTH

Milkweed seeds in October CUB KAHN

Northeast Georgia's fall colors, which usually peak about the third week of October   STEVEN Q. CROY

“ *Here in north Georgia was a rugged section held by hardy people. High up on the plateau at the foot of the Blue Ridge Mountains, she saw rolling red hills wherever she looked, with huge outcroppings of the underlying granite and gaunt pines towering somberly everywhere. It all seemed wild and untamed to her coast-bred eyes accustomed to the quiet jungle beauty of the sea islands. . . .* ”

Margaret Mitchell,
Gone With the Wind

True to their name, the Blue Ridge Mountains—an extension of the Appalachian Mountains—northwest of Gainesville   RALPH DANIEL

An adult and immature bald eagle perched on a snag in Oconee National Forest   JOHN HENDRICKSON

" The winter afternoons glowed with a hazy lemon light and shadows were a delicate blue. . . . and it was said on the day after Christmas that only ten miles to the north there was a light fall of snow. "

Carson McCullers,
The Heart is a Lonely Hunter

Whitetail doe picking her way through one of northern Georgia's short-lived snowfalls   CUB KAHN

Georgia cardinal eyeing snow, which rarely exceeds one inch per year in the state   BATES LITTLEHALES / ANIMALS ANIMALS

A new day coming to Jekyll Island, one of Georgia's coastal playgrounds   CATHERINE KARNOW

> " *. . . purple curtains of the night, and the measured rush of the Atlantic unfurling its huge skirts upon the white sands of the beach . . . resounded through the silent air.* "

Frances Ann Kemble,
Journal of a Residence on
a Georgian Plantation

Shrimp boat sunrise at Savannah   JANEART LTD / THE IMAGE BANK

Stopped by the Atlantic on tiny Tybee Island, which measures five miles long and two miles wide, near Savannah   RALPH DANIEL

Horseshoe crabs coming ashore at high tide at Wolf Island National Wildlife Refuge   JEFF LEPORE

The tip of 10,000-acre Wassaw Island, often called the most beautiful of Georgia's "Golden Isles," surrounded by a silver sea   ROBERT PERRON

Shrimp and commercial fishing boats
at St. Marys   ANDRE JENNY / STOCK SOUTH

Common egret chicks pestering mom
ERWIN & PEGGY BAUER

Watching the passing scenery while picnicking at St. Simons Sound   RALPH DANIEL

The granite top of Kennesaw Mountain, where Sherman viewed Atlanta after his defeat on June 27, 1864   DAVID MUENCH

66 *'Kennesaw smoked and blazed with fire, a volcano as grand as Etna.'* 99

Brother Against Brother,
Time-Life Books

Confederate cannon fire during a re-enactment of the Battle of Kennesaw Mountain   WALTER STRICKLIN / STOCK SOUTH

Confederate calvary, Kennesaw Battlefield re-enactment
WALTER STRICKLIN / STOCK SOUTH

Brotherton Cabin, where Confederate troops charged through Union lines to win the Battle of Chickamauga in 1863   DAVID MUENCH

Cardinal, colorful resident of Georgia's woodlands   KAREN LAWRENCE / STOCK SOUTH

Cardinal flower, whose long, tubular blossoms
are pollinated mainly by hummingbirds   CONNIE TOOPS

Bloodroot, named for the reddish juice in its underground stem,
pushing through oak leaves in Oconee National Forest near Monticello   SCOTT T. SMITH

Young opossum out on a limb   L. WEST

Raccoon at rest in a Georgia pine   JOHN HENDRICKSON

> *"In the strange half-light, the tall pines of the river swamp, so warmly green in the sunshine, were black against the pastel sky, an impenetrable row of black giants hiding the slow yellow water at their feet."*

Margaret Mitchell,
Gone With the Wind

Sunrise on The Pocket, a long peninsula in Okefenokee Swamp   DAVID MUENCH

Golden club blooming in the dark waters of Okefenokee   LARRY R. DITTO

Grinning alligator, flecked with duckweed   ERWIN & PEGGY BAUER

Fragrant water lily, whose blossoms usually open only in the morning and close at midday   EDNA DOUTHAT

Lightning stabbing Ossabaw Island   JOHN M. HALL

" . . . here, thunder and lightning seem as if they might have been invented. Even in winter . . . they appear neither astonishing nor unseasonable, and I should think in summer . . . lightning must be as familiar to these sweltering lands and slimy waters as sunlight itself. "

Frances Ann Kemble,
Journal of a Residence
on a Georgian Plantation

Whitetail doe   WILLIAM S. WEEMS

Smooth yellow violet in Georgia's northern mountains
near the Appalachian Trail   JOHN M. HALL

Harvesting peanuts, Georgia's most valuable crop   WILLIAM BERRY / STOCK SOUTH

Part of the 1.5 billion pounds of peanuts produced annually in Georgia   MICHAEL W. THOMAS / STOCK SOUTH

Georgia tobacco   ANNE HEIMANN

“ *The sun slanted in strong, bronze-colored rays over the green fields. . . . There were acres of tobacco, the plants heavy and green like some monstrous jungle weed. The orchards of peaches with the lush fruit weighting down the dwarfed trees.* ”

Carson McCullers,
The Heart is a Lonely Hunter

Delicious symbols of "The Peach State," near Fort Valley RON SANFORD

> *" The tide's at full: the marsh with flooded streams*
> *Glimmers, a limpid labyrinth of dreams. "*

Sidney Lanier,
Hymns of the Marshes

Adrift in the reflective world of Okefenokee JOHN HENDRICKSON

A narrow waterway framed by
pond cypress and pines, Okefenokee Swamp DAVID MUENCH

Curled fern fronds on the Georgia coast   KEN HAWKINS / STOCK SOUTH

Shells after a storm, Blackbeard Island National Wildlife Refuge   ANDRE JENNY / STOCK SOUTH

Aptly named spider lily, showy flower of southern swamps   JAMES H. ROBINSON

"*This area of brown water lakes, strange moss, huge cypress trees and creeping animals, birds and beasts, is in fact a vast marsh. In spring, it is gorgeous with flowers, but the earth quivers under one's feet.*"

Pearl S. Buck,
Pearl Buck's America

Common egret in Okefenokee, a Seminole Indian word for "land of the trembling earth"   ERWIN & PEGGY BAUER

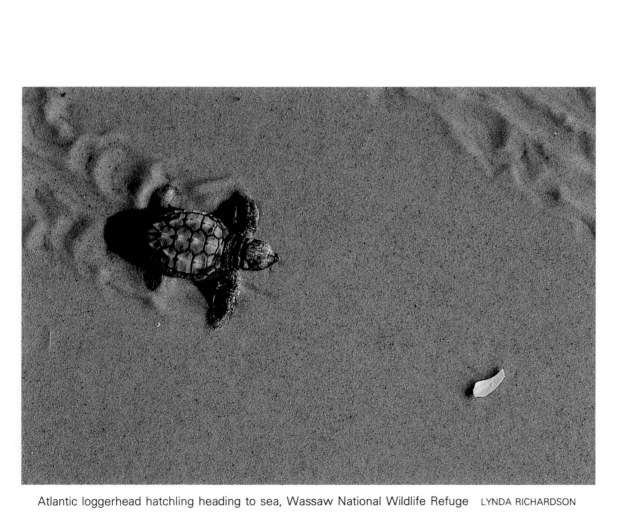

Atlantic loggerhead hatchling heading to sea, Wassaw National Wildlife Refuge   LYNDA RICHARDSON

Shell pattern, Cumberland Island National Seashore   DAVID MUENCH

Purple gallinule, Harris Neck National Wildlife Refuge, one of Georgia's best birding locations   JOHN HENDRICKSON

Copperhead, beautiful but poisonous   STEPHEN G. MAKA / PHOTO NATS

Bald cypress, Spanish moss, and palmetto—three symbols of Georgia's southern coast JOHN HENDRICKSON

Tallulah Canyon, North America's oldest natural gorge, Chattahoochee National Forest   DAVID MUENCH

Flowers of pinesap pipes, one of northern Georgia's most unusual plants, Lake Winfield Scott   DAVID MOLCHOS

“ *Moreover, there was the influence of the Southern physical world—itself a sort of cosmic conspiracy against reality in favor of romance. The country is one of extravagant colors, of proliferating foliage and bloom, of flooding yellow sunlight, and, above all perhaps, of haze.* ”

W. J. Cash,
The Mind of the South

Swamp pink, a threatened member of the lily family   STEVEN Q. CROY

Granite rocks and solution pools at Heggie's Rock, a Nature Conservancy site near Augusta   JEFF LEPORE

" With blood and glory, pride and shame, energy and ideas, Georgians have stitched together a unique and colorful patchwork heritage. "

Zachary A. Kent,
America the Beautiful, Georgia

they made it possible

Georgia on my Mind would have been impossible to produce without the creative and technical skills of more than forty professional photographers. These men and women succeeded in a difficult task—capturing the many moods and faces of the Empire State of the South.

From rugged mountains to majestic seascapes, Georgia contains a breathtaking array of beautiful images, but transforming these images onto film requires more than just a camera. It takes an eye for composition, technical expertise, long hours of work, and the sheer determination to obtain a memorable shot rather than a mere snapshot.

The photographers for *Georgia on my Mind* provided this extra skill and effort. They canoed, hiked, climbed, waited, and watched to get the best possible images from all parts of the state.

To all the excellent photographers who contributed to *Georgia on my Mind*, thank you.

Michael S. Sample,
Bill Schneider
Publishers, Falcon Press

Photographers in *Georgia on my Mind*

Gene Ahrens
Erwin & Peggy Bauer
Annie Griffiths Belt
William Berry
Steve Bisson
Alan D. Briere
Matt Bradley
Flip Chalfant
Willard Clay
John M. Coffman
Ed Cooper
Steven Q. Croy
Scott Cunningham
Ralph Daniel
Larry R. Ditto
Edna Douthat
John Elk III
John M. Hall
Ken Hawkins
Anne Heimann
John Hendrickson

Joey Ivansco
Janeart Ltd.
Andre Jenny
Cub Kahn
Catherine Karnow
Karen Lawrence
Jeff Lepore
Bates Littlehales
Keith Longiotti
Stephen G. Maka
David Molchos
David Muench
David Murray, Jr.
Frank Oberle
David Perdew
Robert Perron
James H. Robinson
Lynda Richardson
Ron Sanford
William Schemmel
Michael A. Schwarz

Laura Sikes
Grafton Marshall Smith
Scott T. Smith
Don Sparks
Walter Stricklin
Michael W. Thomas
Tom Till
Connie Toops
Pat Toops
Larry Ulrich
William S. Weems
L. West

And these photo agencies:
Animals Animals
The Image Bank
Photo/Nats
Photographic Resources
Stock South

acknowledgments

The publishers gratefully acknowledge the following sources:

Pages 8, 16, 32, 46 and 72 from *America the Quotable* by Mike Edelhart and James Tinen. Copyright © 1983 by Mike Edelhart

Pages 14, 64, 78, and 94 from *Gone With the Wind* by Magaret Mitchell. Copyright © 1936 by The MacMillan Company.

Page 20 from *A Good Life in the Low Country* by John J. Putman. Copyright © 1983 by the National Geographic Society.

Page 24 from *Peachtree Road* by Anne Rivers Siddons. Copyright © 1988 by author. Published by Harper & Row.

Page 28 from *Tobacco Road* by Erskine Caldwell. Copyright © 1932 by author. Published by Random House, Inc.

Pages 36 and 38 from *In Search of Our Mothers' Gardens* by Alice Walker. Copyright © 1967 by author. Published by Harcourt Brace Jovanovich.

Page 40 from *The Lost Legacy of Georgia's Golden Isles* by Betsy Fancher. Copyright © 1970 by author. Published by Doubleday & Company, Inc.

Page 43 from *A Thousand-Mile Walk to the Gulf* by John Muir. Copyright © 1916 by Houghton Mifflin Company

Page 51 from *Blue Highways* by William Least Heat Moon. Copyright © 1982 by author. Published by Little, Brown & Company.

Page 56 from *A Place in the Mountains* by Harold H. Martin. Copyright © 1979 by author. Published by Peachtree Publishers, Ltd.

Page 60 from *An Outdoor Journal* by Jimmy Carter. Copyright © 1988 by author. Published by Bantam Books.

Page 62 from *A Good Man is Hard to Find and Other Stories* by Flannery O'Conner. Copyright © 1953 by the author. Published by Harcourt Brace & World, Inc.

Page 74 from *Kenny Rogers' America* by Kenny Rogers. Copyright © 1986 by author. Published by Little, Brown & Company.

Pages 80 and 102 from *The Heart is a Lonely Hunter* by Carson McCullers. Copyright © 1940 by author. Published by Houghton Mifflin Company.

Pages 82 and 98 from *Journal of a Residence on a Georgian Plantation* by Frances Anne Kemble. Copyright © 1961 by Alfred A. Knopf, Inc.

Page 88 from *Brother Against Brother* by Time-Life Books. Copyright © 1990 by Time-Life Books, Inc. Published by Prentice Hall Press.

Page 104 from "Hymns of the Marshes" in *Poems* by Sidney Lanier. Copyright © 1884 by Mary D. Lanier.

Page 108 from *Pearl Buck's America* by Pearl S. Buck. Copyright © 1971 by author and Lyle Kenyon Engel. Published by Bartholomew House Ltd.

Page 115 from *The Mind of the South* by W. J. Cash. Copyright © 1941 by Alfred A. Knopf, Inc.

Page 117 from *America the Beautiful Georgia* by Zachary A. Kent. Copyright © 1988 by Regensteiner Publishing Enterprises, Inc. Published by Childrens Press.

Georgia On My Mind by Hoagy Carmichael and Stuart Gorrell. Copyright © 1930 by Peer International Corporation. Copyright renewed assigned to Peermusic Ltd. International copyright secured. All rights reserved. Used by permission.

about David Bottoms

David Bottoms, the author of the introduction to *Georgia on my Mind*, was born in Canton, Georgia, in 1949. His poems have appeared widely in such magazines as *The Atlantic, The New Yorker, Harper's,* and *The Paris Review*, as well as numerous anthologies. He is the author of three books of poems, *Shooting Rats at the Bibb County Dump, In a U-Haul North of Damascus,* and *Under the Vulture-Tree*. He also has written two novels, *Any Cold Jordan* and *Easter Weekend*. Among his many awards are the Walt Whitman Award of the Academy of American Poets, a National Endowment for the Arts Fellowship, and an Award in Literature from the American Academy and Institute of Arts and Letters. He lives in Atlanta.

Cypress trees at Burns Lake near Valdosta   WALTER STRICKLIN / STOCK SOUTH